I0447932

Editor-in-Chief and Founder:
    Lyndon H. LaRouche, Jr.
Editorial Board: *Lyndon H. LaRouche, Jr. , Helga
    Zepp-LaRouche, Robert Ingraham, Tony
    Papert, Gerald Rose, Dennis Small, Jeffrey
    Steinberg, William Wertz*
Co-Editors: *Robert Ingraham, Tony Papert*
Managing Editor: *Nancy Spannaus*
Technology: *Marsha Freeman*
Books: *Katherine Notley*
Ebooks: *Richard Burden*
Graphics: *Alan Yue*
Photos: *Stuart Lewis*
Circulation Manager: *Stanley Ezrol*

INTELLIGENCE DIRECTORS
Counterintelligence: *Jeffrey Steinberg, Michele
    Steinberg*
Economics: *John Hoefle, Marcia Merry Baker,
    Paul Gallagher*
History: *Anton Chaitkin*
Ibero-America: *Dennis Small*
Russia and Eastern Europe: *Rachel Douglas*
United States: *Debra Freeman*

INTERNATIONAL BUREAUS
Bogotá: *Miriam Redondo*
Berlin: *Rainer Apel*
Copenhagen: *Tom Gillesberg*
Houston: *Harley Schlanger*
Lima: *Sara Madueño*
Melbourne: *Robert Barwick*
Mexico City: *Gerardo Castilleja Chávez*
New Delhi: *Ramtanu Maitra*
Paris: *Christine Bierre*
Stockholm: *Ulf Sandmark*
United Nations, N.Y.C.: *Leni Rubinstein*
Washington, D.C.: *William Jones*
Wiesbaden: *Göran Haglund*

ON THE WEB
e-mail: eirns@larouchepub.com
www.larouchepub.com
www.executiveintelligencereview.com
www.larouchepub.com/eiw
Webmaster: *John Sigerson*
Assistant Webmaster: *George Hollis*
Editor, Arabic-language edition: *Hussein Askary*

EIR (ISSN 0273-6314) *is published weekly
(50 issues), by EIR News Service, Inc.,
P.O. Box 17390, Washington, D.C. 20041-0390.
(703) 777-9451*

European Headquarters: E.I.R. GmbH, Postfach
Bahnstrasse 9a, D-65205, Wiesbaden, Germany
Tel: 49-611-73650
Homepage: http://www.eirna.com
e-mail: eirna@eirna.com
Director: Georg Neudecker

Montreal, Canada: 514-461-1557

Denmark: EIR - Danmark, Sankt Knuds Vej 11,
basement left, DK-1903 Frederiksberg, Denmark.
Tel.: +45 35 43 60 40, Fax: +45 35 43 87 57. e-mail:
eirdk@hotmail.com.

Mexico City: EIR, Sor Juana Inés de la Cruz 242-2
Col. Agricultura C.P. 11360
Delegación M. Hidalgo, México D.F.
Tel. (5525) 5318-2301
eirmexico@gmail.com

Copyright: ©2015 EIR News Service. All rights
reserved. Reproduction in whole or in part without
permission strictly prohibited.

Canada Post Publication Sales Agreement
#40683579

Postmaster: Send all address changes to *EIR*, P.O.
Box 17390, Washington, D.C. 20041-0390.

Signed articles in *EIR* represent the views of the
authors, and not necessarily those of the Editorial
Board.

Manhattan Marches For Mankind

EIR Contents

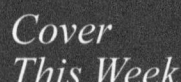

www.larouchepub.com Volume 43, Number 33, August 12, 2016

Cover This Week

A parade in Manhattan celebrating the impending ratification of the U.S. Constitution in 1788.

I. Escalation in Manhattan

LaRouche Acts through Manhattan To Save the Nation

by Dennis Speed

Aug. 8—Lyndon LaRouche has introduced a cultural upshift into his year-long Saturday dialogue with New Yorkers, and two-year organizing initiative known as "the Manhattan Project." The short version would be called: "Think like Einstein." In this way, and only this way, can the American people today live up to the revolution in human affairs, begun by the Founders, that is now required to save this nation in defiance of its apparent electoral or other prospects.

In 1763-1776, the American period of Ben Franklin, George Washington, and Alexander Hamilton, only three and a half million people resided in the thirteen colonies. Within that highly imperfect colonial system, hundreds, perhaps thousands, of great thinkers, inventors, and statesmen were, nonetheless, produced. A self-developing revolutionary form of self-government and physical economy, the greatest in all recorded history, was their monumental creation, advanced by a core of geniuses that included Gottfried Leibniz, who had already been dead for a half century. The Presidency of the United States, a non-hereditary "philosopher king" to be deployed in the service of a Presidential system,— dedicated, as Hamilton's four great Reports on the national bank and its constitutionality, public credit, and manufactures suggest, to ad-

Bringing Hamilton—and the BRICS—to New Yorkers, April 2015.

vance and safeguard the new nation's productive potential for the general welfare of all its people,— was the new system's crown jewel.

Today, with a population of 330 million, about one hundred times that of 1776, can it actually be true that all the United States can presently produce to fill that world-important position, is Hillary Clinton and Donald Trump? The level of political, intellectual, and cultural discourse seen at the recent Democratic and Republican conventions might suggest that to be so, but it is not. Lyndon LaRouche, the world's leading economist (as shown by his 40-year record of successful forecasting), is a part of the institution of the American Presidency. Through his regular Manhattan-based Saturday dialogue session, as well as in smaller, informal discussions with associates, LaRouche has announced to his organization that "I am available," not as a 2016 Presidential candidate, but as a representative of the office of the Presidency, to act as a rallying force capable of removing Obama, and his influence, from provoking World War Three, including thermonuclear war.

LaRouche's institutional role in the United States Presidency was earned much earlier, by dint of the power of the "SDI"—Ronald Reagan's Strategic Defense Initiative—intervention that he made in the late 1970s and early 1980s into world military strategy, nearly defeating the Mutual Assured Destruction (MAD) policy of thermonuclear war. When LaRouche's policy intervention was rejected by the then-Soviet Union of Yuri Andropov, and undermined domestically by circles associated with George Bush "41," George Schultz, Henry Kissinger et al., LaRouche was thrown in jail, after an unsuccessful attempt to assassinate him nearly thirty years ago, on October 6, 1986. Those actions did not stop LaRouche from being correct about the consequences he had forecast for his opponents if they did not adopt his policy.

The Soviet system collapsed as LaRouche had warned them in 1983, by October-November 1989. Within days of the Nov. 9, 1989 fall of the Berlin Wall, LaRouche announced that policy, first termed the "European Triangle," that would over several years, through a "dialogue of cultures," become known as the "Eurasian Land-Bridge," the "New Silk Road," and now the World Land-Bridge.

German banker Alfred Herrhausen's Nov. 30 1989 assassination prevented him from delivering a speech in Manhattan four days later that would have outlined an East-West economic development policy congruent with that of LaRouche, and directly opposite to the now-defunct "Euro" debacle of the past quarter century. Alexander Hamilton would have understood Herrhausen's ideas immediately, and agreed.

The Hamiltonian

LaRouche's Manhattan Project will release this week the first issue of *The Hamiltonian*, reintroducing Americans to Hamilton's economics, and the true idea of the American Presidency, through Lyndon La-

Rouche's intervention on behalf of the American Presidential system. That intervention will not, however, be what you think. It will, proudly, have little to no resemblance to currently acceptable American political practice.

Simultaneous with the release of *The Hamiltonian*, the Schiller Institute will release in New York the proceedings of its June 25-26, 2016 Berlin Conference, "Creating A Common Future for Mankind and a Renaissance of Classical Culture." This conference of 300 participants from 24 nations was keynoted by Helga Zepp-LaRouche, wife of Lyndon LaRouche. The Schiller Institute has, since January 2013, held a series of "New Paradigm" conferences in New York City with the purpose of re-committing Americans to applying Hamilton's economics and Presidential outlook to "win-win" cooperation with the BRICS nations (Brazil, Russia, India, China and South Africa).

Both *The Hamiltonian* and the Berlin Conference report will be distributed in the next days by the Manhattan Project throughout New York City. The Schiller Institute will also be participating in a series of concerts commemorating the fifteenth anniversary of the horrific events of Sept. 11, 2001. The five-week period leading up to that anniversary requires that New Yorkers, who can vividly recall nearly everything about that day, accept their responsibility to end the ongoing coverup by the Obama Administration and the earlier Bush/Cheney Administration of the truth of what was done that day,— of who did it, who did *not* do it, why the nation was intentionally misled, and what is to be done now.

Through this concert series, thousands of New Yorkers are about to create a "living memorial" to those murdered by British and Saudi forces fifteen years ago, in collusion with treasonous elements in the United States itself. This is the only moral way to approach the current American electoral dilemma. The immoral "lesser of two evils" non-choice, for example, is the choice of slaves, not citizens.

On this latter point—the creation of a "living memorial"—New Yorkers have already been ably assisted directly and personally, by Vladimir Putin. More than a decade ago, in 2005, a monument memorializing "9/11" was given to the United States by the government of Russia. Known as "The Teardrop Monument," it is actually called the Monument to the Struggle Against World Terrorism. It represents the two towers of the World Trade Center, violently ripped

wikimedia

The teardrop monument in honor of the victims of 9/11 presented to the United States by Russia. Its official name is: "To the Struggle Against World Terrorism." It is located in Bayonne, New Jersey, where the Statue of Liberty and Manhattan can be seen in the distance. It was dedicated by Russian President Vladimir Putin on Sept. 11, 2006, the fifth anniversary of 9/11.

apart, but united by a gigantic "teardrop of forgiveness."

This 100-foot-tall monument, located in Bayonne, New Jersey, directly across from the former Manhattan site of the Twin Towers and easily visible, is, nonetheless, virtually unknown. Clearly visible to the naked eye from lower Manhattan and Brooklyn, as it was intended to be,— just as is the Statue of Liberty,— no one "sees" it, and few visit it, though hundreds of thousands come to "Ground Zero" regularly.

Putin personally traveled to New Jersey to dedicate the monument at the time. It is unclear whether anyone, other than the city officials of Bayonne itself, has ever

thanked Putin for doing this. (The poster for the upcoming concerts, sponsored by the New York City-based Foundation for the Revival of Classical Culture, features the striking image of the Teardrop Monument.)

The fact that people refuse to see what is standing directly in front of them, whether a 135-ton, 100-foot tall monument, or the win-win new economic platform of Chinese-U.S. economic cooperation, including in space, or the defeat of terrorism through collaboration with Russia and Vladimir Putin—that subjective flaw in American thinking—is about to be overturned by the LaRouche Manhattan project.

The axioms of thought, such as "we have no recourse but to vote for the lesser of two evils," must be overturned, and quickly. A higher standard of American thinking must be provoked, using *The Hamiltonian* and other means, to begin what will be perceived as the most anti-pragmatic, impractical and, to some, unnecessarily baffling of campaigns.

That campaign will put forth the following "outrageous" hypothesis: for a competent, real Presidency to immediately replace the morally hopeless Obama, and the 15-year Obama/Bush attachment of the future of the United States to the irreversibly doomed financial and imperial interests of Britain and Europe's elites, Americans must now quickly learn to "think like Albert Einstein."

He Doesn't Mean What You Think

LaRouche introduced this idea in his Aug. 6 Saturday Manhattan dialogue in a way he had not emphasized before. In response to one questioner who has been consistently active and engaged with people in New York City, but who wanted to know, "what is missing from what we are doing," LaRouche responded:

What's missing is, people do achieve in Manhattan, for example. The population of Manhattan and around its environments is not a pure thing, but it's a good enough thing in terms of functioning as part of the United States as a whole, to make people say, "Yeah, there's something good about this." But the problem is, they don't really get to the point. The point is, what do they have to do?

It's the Einstein principle. Everything depends upon what has been called legitimately "the Einstein principle." The self-development of the individual to understand how the Universe actually responds to the demands of the Universe. That's what Einstein did; and his memory and those who followed him in a deeper way have understood that.

So, the point is, the difference is, trying to qualify for being simply a good fellow, or to simply be a good guy, does not meet that standard. The standard is, you've got to understand what the intention of Einstein was. Now, that's not just that thing in itself. The point is, mankind is a creative force which changes and improves the human species; and that is the difference between what mankind has represented, and the other practical people have represented. Because mankind's ability to create something in itself which goes higher than the existing mankind, is functioning now; that's the issue. And that's where we still tend to fall short.

In a discussion the next day with his associates that comprise his science team, known as "the Basement Team," LaRouche pointed out that when people try to define Einstein, then people who purport to understand him, make mistakes. "Einstein understood himself," LaRouche said. Einstein need not be interpreted: people have to be caused to discover what it is that Einstein has already demonstrated.

Why should no standard lower than this be permissible in an United States Presidential nominee, let alone the elected President? The actual task before the world today is the successful collaboration of Russia, China, the United States, India, Japan, as well as several other nations, charting a bold new future for mankind, including mankind's "extra-terrestrial imperative."

In the exploration of the Moon, the mining of helium-3 there (as now proposed by the Chinese and previously proposed by scientists such as the late Krafft Ehricke) to be used as a fuel in highly energy-dense

LPAC-TV

LaRouche PAC organizers in San Francisco.

power generation, and in the development of a thermonuclear fusion power program on Earth for commercial use over the next fifteen years, we will find mankind at its best. In this way, Einstein's work and its implications can be accessed by millions in America in principle through the space program, just as John F. Kennedy brought ten of millions of Americans into "space consciousness" with his 1962 Rice University speech, setting forth the "impossible" manned Moon missions later called "the Apollo Project."

LaRouche's "Manhattan Project" must now seek to incite that change in thinking that gives people the capacity to think in politics as Einstein thought *as a whole*—not merely in physics, as it is erroneously claimed. Einstein the violinist was the same as Einstein the physicist, Einstein the civil rights activist, Einstein the man. Einstein was a Hamiltonian, in that sense.

The proposed cultural upshift, to have people cure the fault of their misunderstanding of the stars, and therefore of themselves, such "that we are underlings," is the pathway to durable survival that LaRouche has prescribed for the next step of the Manhattan Project. Thinking like the Hamiltonian Einstein, or like the Mozart of the *Requiem*, is the first step to self-qualification of each citizen for the Presidential tasks that lie immediately ahead, including the removal of the threat of thermonuclear war by removing the non-President, Barack Obama, from office, for cause.

Will a President Hillary Clinton Provoke World War III?

by Jeffrey Steinberg

Aug. 4—Within 24 hours of Hillary Clinton's formal nomination as the Democratic Party's 2016 presidential candidate, some of Clinton's top foreign policy and national security campaign advisers came out with blood-curdling attacks against Russia and against Syrian President Bashar al-Assad.

Even as the Democratic Convention was underway, former CIA Director and Defense Secretary under Barack Obama, Leon Panetta, told the convention on July 27 that the key to ending the Syrian war is to overthrow President Assad. Two days later, Jeremy Bash, Panetta's former chief of staff at CIA and the Pentagon and now a top adviser to Clinton, told the *Daily Telegraph* that one of Clinton's first actions as President would be to order a top-down review of Syria policy, with the goal of putting the ouster of Assad at the top of the priorities. He argued that there is no prospect of defeating the Islamic State and Jabhat al-Nusra without removing Assad.

Michèle Flournoy, who is viewed as Hillary Clinton's top choice to be Secretary of Defense, told *Defense One* that a new administration must create a "no bomb zone" in the north of Syria, to safe-house rebel fighters and train and arm them to overthrow Assad, as well as to combat ISIS and

World Economic Forum/swiss-image.ch/
Remy Steinegger

Al-Nusra. She advocated the use of stand-off weapons—guided missiles which can be launched from sufficient distance to protect the attackers from defensive action—against the Syrian Army as another escalation in the regime-change war launched against Syria by President Obama and Secretary of State Clinton in early 2011.

Flournoy is the CEO of the Center for a New American Security (CNAS), a think-tank dominated by Clinton advisers and other neoconservatives. Flournoy's interview with *Defense One* was a condensed version of a report CNAS had just produced from its ISIS Study Group, which included a collection of war-hawks and neocons who are all part of the Clinton stable: Ryan Crocker, Kimberly Kagan, Joseph Lieberman, Gen. David Petraeus, Kenneth Pollack, Andrew Tabler, and Frances Townsend.

In May, CNAS had published a blueprint for global confrontation, called "Extending American Power: Strategies to Expand American Engagement in a Com-

Left, Former Secretary of State Hillary Clinton is shown testifying before the House Select Committee on Benghazi. She has declared herself the "continuity" candidate from the nearly two decades of wars in Afghanistan and Iraq extending from former Vice President Dick Cheney (top) and President Obama (center).

wikimedia

petitive World Order," which was co-authored by Robert Kagan, a leading neocon who prepared a similar study for the incoming Bush-Cheney Administration in 2000, the "Project for a New American Century." Both documents advanced a unipolar world based on projection of ever-expanding U.S. military power. The PNAC study was widely seen as the game-plan that Bush and Cheney used to launch the decade of permanent wars in Afghanistan and Iraq,— a game-plan later extended by Obama and Clinton into Syria and Libya.

Following the diatribes by Panetta, Bash, and Flournoy, many astute observers concluded that the attacks on Syria, Russia, and China which were included in their combined remarks, could not have been issued without prior approval by Hillary Clinton herself.

In short, Clinton has declared herself as the "continuity" candidate from the nearly two decades of permanent war launched by Bush and Obama. Those wars have now put the world on the verge of thermonuclear war with Russia and China,— a war that will wipe out humankind.

While serving as Secretary of State, Hillary Clinton was one of the most strident advocates of war and more war in the Obama Administration. Clinton was and remains a strong promoter of the need to overthrow the Assad government in Damascus, through direct U.S. military involvement if necessary. Her demand to create a no-fly zone inside Syrian territory is a blatant violation of all principles of national sovereignty, and her role in the launching of the disastrous Libyan war— widely described as the decisive vote in the rush to regime-change—has created a permanent crisis through-

One of Clinton's first actions as President would be to order a top-down review of the Syria policy, with the goal of putting the ouster of Assad at the top of the priorities.

CSIS/CC
Jeremy Bash

DoD/Chad J. McNeeley, U.S. Navy
Leon E. Panetta

CNAS/JaRel Clay/CC
Michèle Flournoy

'Hillary ought to be ashamed of herself for being herself'— Lyndon LaRouche

Aug. 5—In recent discussions with associates in the wake of the Democratic Convention in Philadelphia, Lyndon LaRouche said of Hillary Clinton, "She is not a winning figure. Nor is he [Trump]. The only thing they can do is to cause doom. They cannot win, except by causing doom." He went on to describe Hillary Clinton as "a professional stooge for Obama," who is running a "swindle against the people of the United States." He said that she is on the edge of "going down as a political figure." LaRouche identified the starting point of that doom as the moment on July 13, 2015, when LaRouche PAC organizer Daniel Burke asked Hillary Clinton at a Manhattan event whether she would act to reinstate Glass-Steagall. "He insisted that he get an answer, and she refused. She's just making more and more enemies," LaRouche said.

LaRouche further emphasized that someone has to identify what caused Obama to become President of the United States, and pointed to the role of British Empire operator George Soros. He said, "Obama is an instrument of this body." Hillary has made herself a tool of the same British Empire that runs Obama, by her decision to support him. Hillary Clinton has been identified as the instigator of the Obama Administration's 2011 bombing of Libya, and the subsequent murder of its President Muammar Gaddafi. She later wittingly lied about the cause of the Sept. 11, 2012 terrorist attack on the U.S. Consulate in Benghazi, which resulted in the deaths of four American citizens, including Ambassador Chris Stevens.

—Diane Sare

out the African continent, leading to mass deaths and social chaos.

It was Hillary Clinton, along with Susan Rice and Samantha Power, who pushed for the ouster of Libyan leader Qaddafi, even though it meant aligning with hard-core Al-Qaeda and related jihadist terror groups. The overthrow and assassination of Qaddafi turned Libya into an ungovernable no-man's-land, run by warring cliques of heavily armed militias, many dominated by Al-Qaeda in the Islamic Maghreb (AQIM) and subsequently by the Islamic State.

Nuland's Nazis

The weapons that were "liberated" from Libyan government stockpiles have fueled wars across the African continent, and large quantities of those "loose weapons" were smuggled into Syria, through U.S., British, Saudi Arabian, Qatari and Turkish channels, into the hands of the jihadists who have turned Syria and Iraq into a Hell on Earth. Millions of refugees from the North African, Syrian, Iraqi, and Afghan conflicts, all boosted by Obama and Clinton, have flooded into Western Europe in desperate flight for their lives, creating the biggest refugee crisis in the entire postwar period.

Hillary Clinton's four years as Secretary of State for Barack Obama, led directly to the events of Sept. 11, 2012, when jihadists from Ansar al-Sharia staged a heavily-armed assault on the U.S. diplomatic compound in Benghazi, Libya, resulting in the murder of U.S. Ambassador Christopher Stevens and three other American officials.

As State Department documents detailed, for months prior to the Benghazi 9/11 attack, Ambassador Stevens and other U.S. diplomats in Libya had begged for increased security personnel. The State Department compiled a grid of scores of attacks on foreign diplomats and even the International Red Cross, but secu-

Clinton, along with Susan Rice and Samantha Power, pushed for the ouster of Libyan leader Qaddafi, even though it meant aligning with hard-core Al-Qaeda and related jihadist terror groups.

Libyan rebels' photostream
Men flee as Qaddafi's tent burns behind them, Tripoli, Aug. 24, 2011.

UN/Manuel Elías
US Representative to the UN Samantha Power.

Susan Rice, Obama
Administration National
Security Adviser.
UN/Devra Berkowitz

rity was actually stripped, rather than boosted. While State Department official Patrick Kennedy was ostensibly in charge of security arrangments for the U.S. diplomatic mission in Libya, the buck really stopped with the Secretary—Hillary Clinton.

As the Benghazi attack on 9/11/12 was unfolding, live reports from Benghazi and from the embassy in Tripoli made clear that the attack on the mission was premeditated, well-planned, heavily armed, and deadly. A Defense Intelligence Agency assessment, released within the government days after the attack, spelled out precisely how the attack was conducted.

Yet, President Obama and Secretary of State Clinton, more concerned with the upcoming November 2012 presidential elections, chose to lie to the American people and claimed that the attack in Benghazi was a "spontaneous" protest against a little-known video slandering the Prophet Mohammed—a baldfaced lie.

Clinton, along with her trusted State Department ally, Victoria Nuland, created a total confrontation with Russia, which, at critical moments, put her in bed with outright Nazis.

CC/tandalov.com

Anti-government protesters at Maidan Square in Kiev, Ukraine, January 22, 2014.

That lie, worked out in a late-night phone call between President Obama and Secretary Clinton, and first issued to the public in a press release issued under Clinton's name, was maintained for days. On the Sunday after the attack, National Security Adviser Susan Rice went on a string of interview shows to peddle the "spontaneous protest gone wild" lie, first issued by Clinton.

CC/Mariusz Kubik

Victoria Nuland, Assistant Secretary of State for European and Eurasian Affairs.

Hillary Clinton put the re-election of Barack Obama ahead of the truth and the vital national security interests of the United States. She calculated that if she had told the truth and resigned from the Administration, Obama would have been defeated for re-election, she would have been blamed, and her own future prospects of being Presidential nominee of the Democratic Party would have been ended.

Lyndon LaRouche presented the case against Hillary Clinton and Barack Obama in an historic press conference in Washington, D.C. at the National Press Club in the weeks following the Benghazi tragedy. LaRouche identified Clinton as a stooge for Obama and as a leading member of the war party, that has given the United States and the world the longest-running perpetual war, has created the conditions for the rise of the Islamic State, and has bankrupted the U.S. economy.

Hillary Clinton not only presided over the rise of ISIS and the total destabilization of the entire Middle East/North Africa region. She, along with her trusted State Department ally, Victoria Nuland, created a total confrontation with Russia, which, at critical moments, put her in bed with outright Nazis.

Clinton promoted Nuland, the wife of neocon ideologue Robert Kagan, to top State Department posts, from spokeswoman for Secretary Clinton and the Department, to Assistant Secretary of State for European and Eurasian Affairs. From that post, Nuland presided over the "color revolution" which overthrew the Yanukovych government in Ukraine, using assets from the Banderist Nazi apparatus, which had fought side-by-side with Hitler's armies during World War II,— and then spawned several generations of avowed neo-Nazis like the Ukrainian Right Sector and Azov Brigades.

At one crucial moment in the overthrow of Yanukovych, Nuland boasted to an audience at the National Press Club in Washington that the United States had spent $5 billion on the Ukraine "democracy" campaign since the breakup of the Soviet Union.

That 2013-2014 *coup d'état* in Kiev marked the dramatic escalation of the Obama Administration's already ongoing provocations against Russian President Vladimir Putin, actions that now include the deployment of NATO forces on the borders of Russia for the first time since the Nazi invasion of the Soviet Union in World War II.

It was Obama and Clinton, joined at the hip, who destroyed the United States-Russian relationship, and have now put the world on a dangerous course towards general war, and even potentially a thermonuclear war of extinction. This is the real Obama-Clinton legacy.

Hillary Clinton detests the fact that Lyndon LaRouche has fearlessly made the truth of her record available to the American people and the world.

Einstein's Model: The Best Choice for Mankind's General Self-Development

This is an edited transcript of a dialogue between Lyndon H. LaRouche, Jr. and the Manhattan Project, on Saturday, Aug. 6, 2016.

Dennis Speed: My name is Dennis Speed, and on behalf of the LaRouche Political Action Committee I want to welcome you here for the Aug. 6 dialogue with Lyndon LaRouche. And we have Lyndon LaRouche with us today [applause] as you can see. So, I think the best thing to do is to ask Mr. LaRouche if he has an opening statement; and then from there, we go right into our questions and answers, since I'm sure he's eager to get to that. So, Lyn?

Lyndon LaRouche: Well, I think the immediate question is how we in Manhattan in particular—but also in adjoining areas—are going to be able to mobilize the population the way we have to. I think what we've got right here before us, is a relatively significant population. There probably could be more, or probably will be more in the same room. But I think the important thing is to lay out the souls of people. I don't mean by wild ideas and things. I mean just the idea to address what you really believe in, and what you can justify in believing in. That, I think, is the standard for discovery of truth.

Speed: Very good. So, let's go right to our first question.

China Discovers its Soul

Renee Sigerson: Good afternoon. It's actually a very exciting time, because this bad performance, this boring and bad performance called the election campaign is going through a natural death right now, and clearing the air. People are becoming accessible to discussing what we really have to do, as opposed to that bad Broadway hit, "Who You Gonna Vote For? Who You Gonna Vote For?" which is really completely ridiculous under these circumstances.

> The standard which came into being, during and following the founding of the Einstein system, has given us a higher level, a more accurate level of understanding what mankind is.

Diane pointed out last night that only 9% of the American adult population had anything to do with the primary process that was the hullabaloo before these conventions, which—thank God—have now ended. I'm finding there's a really notable change in the way that people are responding to us, but that you have to know how to get at it. I'm going to ask you to comment on the difference between approaching organizing from the standpoint of an agenda, versus a mission, because what I'm finding is that when you first start talking to somebody, they're really pent up with withdrawal from the world, because they're so overwhelmed by what's going on. So, if you begin to discuss a predicate with people—this particular thing—they just can't respond and they want to get off the phone. They're too busy; they have to get to work; the coffee just burned in the coffee pot; this kind of thing. But if you approach people from the highest level, which is that we're reaching everybody because we are going to completely change the agenda on a worldwide basis, that we're in touch with people all over the world, that on Tuesday morning, we're hitting the street with a new newspaper that with its lead article is going to destroy Hillary Clinton .... And we want to talk to them about being part of a mission which is to change the entire agenda in the United States,— all of a sudden, they have time and they're interested. They start asking questions. You find that people really are struggling—and a lot of the population today is very under-educated—struggling to understand how you deal with something like this.

I could go through a lot of details about this, but I think the point is made clearly enough by what I've said. It's actually quite shocking to see the change that goes on in conversation with people if you approach it from that high level, as opposed to trying to appeal to them about an issue. I wonder if you would comment on that.

LaRouche: Sure! Glad to do so. The point is, Ein-

Chinese leader Deng Xiaoping and his wife Zhuo Lin (right) being briefed by Johnson Space Center Director Christopher C. Kraft (extreme right) Feb. 2, 1979.

stein. The standard which came into being, during and following the founding of the Einstein system, has given us a higher level, a more accurate level of understanding what mankind is. That standard tells you better than anything else,— to the extent it's a self-standing operation,— it's the most authoritative thing you can do in self-examination.

Follow-up to question: Okay. Let me just take that one step further. In discussing what we're doing internationally with people, you find that the attacks on Putin really don't work. Some people will even say, "I think he's better than anybody we've had in the Presidency for a long time." People can see the difference, but there's a poorer understanding of China.

There's a very interesting story about what really happened in China when Mao Zedong died and Deng Xiaoping took over, and Americans have no understanding whatsoever of what happened. To say it in brief—it's a longer discussion in depth—but to say it in brief, the success of what Deng Xiaoping did, seems to

me to be based on the fact that he was seeking an answer to this question of how to increase the productivity of the economy, that this was the foremost thing that was on his mind. It really made me think of how this question of productivity, also right now in the United States itself is so important. This is not unrelated to what you just said about Einstein, but I wonder if you would say something further about this question of productivity.

LaRouche: Well, the problem is obvious. China was being victimized by being self-subjected to conditions in which the nation as a whole were victims. What happened is, China discovered its own soul. I don't say that China has fully discovered its own soul, but I think it's done an excellent job on this so far. Particularly as in contrast to Obama. If you want to get a comparison, try Obama; and Obama is a failure at becoming a successful Satan. He wants to be Satan, but he doesn't make the quality; he doesn't have it.

What's Missing

Question: Hi, Lyn. Alvin here in New York. It's kind of two parts here that I want to run through with you. What I'm experiencing so far in conversations and having people sign the petition, people who have been generally one would kindly call "non-political"; I've used this petition to engage them. On the surface, there's no problem getting signatures, none whatsoever. Of course, it's in going through the leaflet with them and what the deeper implications are of it, what our intentions are, and what's required; then they're forced to think, not just sign. "Oh sure. The 28 pages are great; they should be released." And it makes them think more about what their responsibility should actually become.

So, on the one hand it has been easy, but on the other hand, it really is forcing people to think. It's bringing them into some realm of reality, should they decide that they want to be a part of reality.

The second thing I wanted to share with you, was that last week, over the weekend, the Schiller Institute had a concert in Spanish Harlem. I think this was a significant advancement of the Manhattan Project. The gentleman who was the leader of this community-based group has been in Spanish Harlem his entire life, and to his knowledge this was the first time that any Classical music had been performed there. So, as we and as I work toward building the audience for the series of concerts on Sept. 11, I thought that this was a significant event. It was a very good start for what we're looking to do.

So, with those two things, the question to you is, are we on the right track with this? And is this enough? Is this going to work? Or, put another way, what's missing in what we should be doing here in New York?

LaRouche: The latter—what's missing. What's missing is, people do achieve in Manhattan, for example; the population of Manhattan and around its environments is not a pure thing, but it's a good enough thing in terms of functioning as part of the United States as a whole, to make people say, "Yes, there's something good about this." But the problem is, they don't really get to the point. The point is, what do they have to do? It's the Einstein principle, because everything depends upon what has been called legitimately the Einstein principle. The self-development of the individual to understand how the Universe actually responds to the demands of the Universe. That's what Einstein did, and those who followed him in a deeper way have understood that.

So, the point is, the difference in trying to simply qualify to be a good fellow, or to simply be a good guy, does not meet that standard. The standard is, you've got to understand what the intention of Einstein was. Now, that's not just that thing in itself. The point is, mankind is a creative force which changes and improves the human species. And that is the difference between what mankind represented, and the other practical people have represented. Because mankind's ability to create something in itself which goes higher than the existing level mankind is functioning at now,— that's the issue. And that's where we still tend to fall short. We can start fixing that right now.

Diane Sare: My question is, we actually came up with this idea of the 9/11 Living Memorial at a meeting here some months ago, when Patrick

> The Einstein principle: The self-development of the individual to understand how the Universe actually responds to the demands of the Universe. That's what Einstein did, and those who followed him in a deeper way have understood that.

> Einstein's intention: mankind is a creative force which changes and improves the human species.... Because mankind's ability to create something in itself which goes higher than the existing level mankind is functioning at now,— that's the issue.

asked you about the people who had died—the veterans and the first responders and so on. And now we are only five weeks away from a series of concerts, the Mozart *Requiem* performances. We have had a lot more people killed worldwide since that time, in all of these various terrorist attacks and mass shooting attacks which are, I guess you could call it, "cultural terrorism"—if it's not coordinated out of Saudi Arabia, it's coordinated out of Silicon Valley, with the new violence and the video games.

So, I've had a certain idea of these concerts, something like what Putin did in Palmyra, where you're demonstrating a commitment to a certain principle of humanity over barbarism and transforming the population. But I just wanted to get your thoughts now, because I think the situation is extremely intense in terms of the purpose and the direction in the way we should be organizing and planning for this series of Mozart's Requiem concerts.

Roosevelt's Contribution

LaRouche: That's a very important thing. Because this was of course, on the edge of his [Mozart's] own death, which was actually largely induced, induced by force of malice from outside.

But what he did in his religious devotions,— which are the most important, most significant thing of all of his work, and when people get into those motions, those arcs, and are able to sing that kind of music, then something happens to them. And it's comparable in a sense, to Beethoven. Beethoven was a different kind of person in many respects. That is, his muscular power of the mind was something unique. But actually there's very little difference morally between one and the other. They both have a part of the same heritage and intention, and that's what you can work with.

People should just work with that. I mean working with Einstein, working with the musical leaders, are all the same thing. They are the self-directing development of the human individual, and that's what it is.

It's a good way to go. There are

other ways to go which are also useful and comparably so. But that is the thing I suggest, really is the way to go, particularly when music is present.

Question: Hi Mr. LaRouche, this is R— from Bergen County, New Jersey. The Reconstruction Finance Corporation from the days of the Depression, it seems to me, was absolutely essential to saving people and bringing some sanity back into the economic system, and of course that is coupled with the Glass-Steagall. It seems to me at this point, that with the Glass-Steagall on both of the Party platforms, that in some sense it has entered into the consciousness at least of some people. Do you think we've reached a point that we do more to strongly link up the Glass-Steagall with the idea of a national credit bank, and that if we don't establish a national credit bank, the United States is really going to sink, it's really going to be bad? That it is absolutely essential at this point? What is your feeling on that?

LaRouche: Absolutely. This was Franklin Roosevelt's contribution to the future of mankind. And I had some indirect contact with him, because I was associated with people in the leadership of the President's functions, and therefore, by knowing these people and having an indirect connection to them, I came to understand what the Franklin Roosevelt principle really meant as such.

And so, therefore, we really should simply understand that what the model of Franklin Roosevelt represents is something which people should use as a likely way of bringing out in them, some of those kinds of development which Franklin Roosevelt represented in his own way.

Question: Good afternoon Mr. LaRouche, speaking as G— from Queens, New York. And my question is about one of the handouts from LaRouche PAC which has to do with exposing 9/11. And in the back of the handout we have five demands; and the first demand was to disclose or declassify the 28 pages, and we check that off the list. And it says that the 28 pages can help to reveal the Anglo-Saudi apparatus which supported the 9/11 hijackers. Now, the second demand is the public disclosure of the "Al-Yamamah" weapons for petroleum deal negotiated by then British Prime Minister Margaret Thatcher and Saudi Prince Bandar. Now, the Al-Yamamah deal is the weapons for petroleum deal "which created the sufficient off-the-books finances needed for the 9/11 attacks."

My question to you is how difficult would it be to go from step 1 to check off step 2? To declassify the Al-Yamamah deal?

LaRouche: Well, first of all, the whole package which I had some firsthand experience with, together with some people in Britain who shared my view—they were not treated as nicely, as the British citizens of relevance. But the main thing about this is the British Empire has always been since its beginning, as a beginning, has been a Satanic operation. It has been intrinsically Satanic. And what's happened is the effect of that kind of culture, and the fact that people try to get by, by satisfying the demands of that culture,— that is the way in which many people of the United States have lost their souls. They're still running around, they look the same way, somewhat, except the bad faces on their attitudes. But the point is, that's it. This is something we have to cope with, because that is exactly what we have to examine in ourselves, or in general.

The Case of India

Question: Good evening Mr. LaRouche. I am looking at what I call a "cross-Atlantic apocalypse" right now. On the eastern side of the Atlantic, the British central bank just cut interest rates for the first time in seven years. Italy's economy is at the crossroads with Greece. And Deutsche Bank is drowning in toxic derivatives. On this side of the Atlantic, the western side, we have almost no real choice politically speaking. The U.S. economy as far as it is reported this morning, is household consumer-driven but not investment driven. In between, we have the Caribbean region which is dependent on tourism, from both of these sides, on export agriculture, and also on remittances, which account for up to 43% in some cases. The future outlook for this region looks very grim.

My question to you is, what basket of strategies do you think, both social and financial, is needed for us to steer free in the near future?

LaRouche: Well, take the case of India, which is a relevant case for this discussion; and therefore we have to understand what the good has been in each of the cultures which have dominated at certain times and beyond. Now, that's the starting point, but we always have to look out for a further starting point, not just that. We have to find out a higher level of starting point than the one which is culturally characteristic of any culture or subculture.

And so it's that desire to create, the sense of the

need to create, to create in mankind, the living mankind, the living population,— to achieve something which that mankind heretofore has not actually achieved. Therefore the idea of the self-achievement within the culture of the particular kinds of cultures, of languages and so forth, these things all come together as one mix. This is what is the history is, from my standpoint—and I had a lot of experience with India at times, and other things, and I've seen this. But it comes down to the fact, if you have the kind of commission, self-commission to yourself, to discover a higher order of achievement in your own characteristic population, the adopted one, and if you find that you are able to improve on the effect of that culture as it is developed, then you are making progress, and you are making progress for mankind.

Question: Mr. LaRouche it's good to see you. This is H— from New York. Actually, I have my child here today, and we were discussing a certain summer camp that has certain leftist—both good points and bad points. Anyway, they were discussing a story about the Quechua Indians who live in Ecuador and this area in South America, and they were forced to give up their oil to China, and also there were demonstrations against the government in Ecuador, which were probably some effects that were not even something that they knew about.

The problem is that people get caught up in these stories that involve justice both in the United States and other countries. And how does a young person know if they're true or not, in general, when we get these stories about the oppressed and so forth?

India and Einstein

LaRouche: Well, I don't think you can really take it from that standpoint. I think these are—fetishes, really, in effect.

> It's that desire to create, the sense of the need to create ... in mankind, ... [the need] to achieve something which that mankind heretofore has not actually achieved. Therefore the idea of the self-achievement within the culture of the particular kinds of cultures, of languages and so forth, these things all come together as one mix.

> What's important is what mankind can achieve in mankind's own person; that's the real thing. Therefore, you have to have an object, that is an object of mission, and that mission becomes your dominant interest; and that's what we have to do. We have to actually improve mankind. We do that by thinking, not of what we can do for ourselves, or do in ourselves, but what we can do in and for the people around us.

What's important is what mankind can achieve in mankind's own person; that's the real thing. Now, therefore, you have to have an object, that is an object of mission, and that mission becomes your dominant interest; and that's what we have to do. We have to actually improve mankind. We do that by thinking, not of what we can do for ourselves, or do in ourselves, but what we can do in and for the people around us.

That's the real issue. And that's the only way you can really achieve that. It's creation of the other people, of the people with other cultures, who need to bring cultures together in a certain way.

Now, look at what's happened in China. China is a great power right now. In every moral sense, and somewhat beyond, China is a great power, and has become a great power through the leadership of leading Chinese figures in their process. This is one of the great building blocks for a future mankind, for all mankind—just as other parts of the world, outside of that of China's culture, have similar destinies available to them. They may not practice that, but they have something available to them that will do that.

And so therefore you have to rejoice in the fact that you have helped to create a higher level of development and achievement of the human species. That is what makes you happy.

Avneet Thapar: Hi Lyn, because you brought up India and Einstein, it provokes a question in my mind, because in the earlier 20th Century it was very clear to a lot of Indian patriots and leading thinkers that the way to alleviate India's condition was not just being anti-British—it had to be more; that India had to develop a real identity and had to be a place where you can say, the "East meets the West." So Tagore, who was a leading Indian thinker and philosopher, and a Nobel Prize winner—Tagore in various letters to Einstein and others

> **In every moral sense, and somewhat beyond, China is a great power, and has become a great power through the leadership of leading Chinese figures in their process. This is one of the great building blocks for a future mankind, for all mankind—just as other parts of the world, outside of that of China's culture, have similar destinies available to them.**

brought that up, that it is through science that we are going to unite humanity together around a higher purpose. So, I just wanted your thoughts on that.

LaRouche: Well, simply, the great problem in India has been, insofar as I know India,— and I have a considerable amount of experience with India, either directly or indirectly. I spent a good deal of time in India. So you see, what is it that sometimes makes some of the population of India self-destructive? Certain family practices which are induced, which are destructive?

Now, these things are not necessary. This is not a natural thing. This is a self-destruction. For example, education in India in former times, education of an individual Indian citizen, child: These things were things which the adult population, or many parts of the adult population, do not really comprehend. Because the question is not how to be servile, or how to achieve according to a fixed standard. The point is, can an Indian for example, rise to an achievement to teach some of their own family in terms of culture? That is, by looking at ways to find out how to create advances in the quality of culture. And this has happened in some cases in China, and it's happened in India; where the general problem up to now, is that we have to make sure that all governments, all nations, have access to that kind of self-improvement.

It's the self-improvement, not what they get, but the self-improvement, that makes their life worthwhile.

Xinhua

China's Experimental Fusion Reactor EAST.

Question follow-up: Thanks. That's a lot to think about.

Question: Good afternoon, Mr. LaRouche, this is S— from Harlem. I just got back from a month-long trip in China. I visited five different cities, had a chance to see all their cultural elements: museums, gardens, the railway system. It's all wonderful. And anyone that's espousing that China's having some sort of economic slowdown, there's no proof of that from what I saw.

LaRouche: China is a real revolution, in and of itself. And the creation of the current administration of China is a marking feature of what China has accomplished by self-development of China as a nation. That's true, that's important. And that's something that Chinese people can, and do largely, represent. That's their attitude, that's their outlook. And you find out, you know, the development of China's role in this current role, is really a very creative one. It has a very strong value for all nations, and it's going to grow. It's going to get bigger, that is, in that way; better in that way.

Yes, China really is a miracle right now.

Question follow-up: Something else I also found out is that the government is pro-actively helping the population re-embrace Confucianism. All the places that were destroyed during the Cultural Revolution, they've rebuilt them. They're actually helping out, basically rekindling the flame of Confucianism within the country. And also the whole ban on Facebook and Google in China,— what you can do, is use a personal VPN, and you can get Facebook and Google and the country doesn't persecute you for it. So it's not that they don't want their people to have the information or the access, I think it's on the other side: they don't want Facebook and Google to have access to their population.

Xinhua/Liu Junxi

This photo (taken April 25, 2016) shows the ion cyclotron resonant heating (ICRH) antenna, a key part of a nuclear fusion facility, at the Chinese Academy of Sciences Institute of Plasma Physics (ASIPP) in Hefei, China. This world-class ICRH antenna, manufactured by ASIPP, was delivered to a French institute in Anhui Province.

Einstein People

LaRouche: I think the leadership in China, presently, in the present regime and in the present actions, and its relationship to Russia, these things and other things as well ... India tends to be drawn into closer affinity with China. And there are more instances of that.

The root of the matter is the principle of action by which nations develop themselves. When you see the self-development process of a nation, and you find that it is a good one and that it works, as China today in comparison to some of the things that China experienced earlier. It's all there. And this is what defines mankind.

You know, this is the Einstein principle that I'm talking about. Einstein is probably the leading genius in all modern history, because of what he did. As a matter of fact, he's still doing it. He's been dead for over a generation, but he is still creating and generating into the population a great movement for progress of the human mind.

So this self-development of the human mind, as the human mind, simply as the human mind,— and the question is are you going to be a participant in the self-development of the

> **The root of the matter is the principle of action by which nations develop themselves. When you see the self-development process of a nation, and you find that it is a good one and that it works, as China today in comparison to some of the things that China experienced earlier. It's all there. And this is what defines mankind.**

human mind? That I think is the best example of what has to be done.

Elliot Greenspan: Hi Lyn. We in the Manhattan Project are in the middle of a national Presidential campaign, which certainly would qualify as the most fraudulent, and potentially tragic campaign in the history of the country. It needs a new ingredient, and what you have made clear since Sunday, is that your intention is to shape a new Presidency. You have a moment, as Helga emphasized in her speech in Beijing a few days ago, a combination of crises, perhaps unparalleled,— but we have new paradigm, which you and she have helped to shape, and have initiated over decades. There was a crucial point that was made by one of our organizers a couple of days ago, in discussion, which she's emphasizing in her discussions with supporters, that perhaps the last time there was a sovereign decision, a sovereign policy initiative made by an American President, was March 23, 1983, when Reagan put forward the Strategic Defense Initiative—your policy, your idea, a campaign which you had initiated several years earlier. And she was saying this in part, because people get totally wrapped up, or much of the electorate is wrapped up in the "lesser of evils," as they might think of it. These are evil. But policy is made, in general, above the President; it's made within the institution of the Presidency, or it's made by ideas and by thinkers, as you have exemplified.

My question, which I think would be valuable for the participants in the Manhattan Project who will hit the streets by Tuesday with *The Hamiltonian*, with this new publication that we're about to unleash,— it would be valuable, I think, for people to have your insight and input into the process by which you and the Policy Committee and the rest of us, have the challenge and opportunity to shape and create a new Presidency, over this 100-day period. That's my question.

> This is the Einstein principle that I'm talking about. Einstein is probably the leading genius in all modern history, because of what he did, this self-development of the human mind, and the question is: Are you going to be a participant in the self-development of the human mind? That I think is the best example of what has to be done.

> We should consider ourselves as in a march, a march for victory, a victory for mankind; a victory for the United States, a victory for the future of mankind in general. And for achieving things as people, which mankind has never successfully done well, so far.

LaRouche: Well, I think the Einstein model is probably the best choice of model for mankind's self-development, and this is a general self-development, not just for some people. And the lack of that kind of development among our people, is the source of the greatest weakness shared among the people generally.

But that idea, the Einstein conception: Why? See, people think that human beings are born as babies, just simply as babies. They think that the baby naturally is human, and that the baby will behave according to a naturally human development of progress. Well, that isn't true.

The fact is, what happens is whole cultures, or sections of cultures, have shown, by Einstein's effort and by the consequences of this effort, that mankind is capable chiefly, of coming to an understanding of the building of whole hordes of people who are creative. And these are people who are really Einstein people. That is, that they were not trained in simple ways; they really developed a commitment inside themselves, to become really, truly, creative human beings.

And that is the thing that most people fail to understand: What is it that makes a human being creative? And I think most people don't know what that means.

We're on a March

Judy Clark: I think that would be the best place to end the discussion, but I've been asked to say a couple of words about a wonderful day we had in Manhattan midweek. Some of our most loyal and patriotic adherents to your leadership in Manhattan, most of them over 65, like myself, some over 70, came out into the streets in just a couple of hours at midday, very near our location here where our meetings are; and just greeted fellow citizens on their way to the grocery store, on their way to the subway, on their way to the doctor, and we found a resonance that I think surprised each of us, delightfully. When we said, "we've got a petition here that Mr. LaRouche is circulating in his own name to beguile you into taking your Manhattan identity back and fighting for a future, that neither Hillary nor any other candidate you've seen," since you've run, Lyndon, for the office of the Presidency, has upheld. And that we're rallying around the injustice of 9/11 and the breakthrough that's finally been made in opening up those 28 pages, and we led that fight, and Sen. Richard Black from Virginia said that in his own words, recently here, in a dialogue that we participated in with him; that it was "the LaRouche forces who have led this relentlessly."

And so when we presented them a petition that says, "we're going to achieve justice all the way on this, and we're going to work with Russia, and we're going to fight these bloody terrorists, and we're going to bring justice back."... And we've tapped into something: There were octogenarian professors and people in the arts, and retired door-men, and so forth, and all of them,— you know, you get your weakling, who says, "ohhh, that's LaRouche..." And then they're trying to remember why they don't like LaRouche, and then you say, "He's the one that the Bushes put in jail because he's been fighting against these stupid wars his whole life, since he fought against Hitler..." and then they go, "Oh? Okay!" and then, you know, you can just blow away decades of decadence and degeneration and tragedy by stepping forth as you have done with us now, to say, "Well, we're planting the guidon and we are going to win this one."

LaRouche: *Sehr gut!* Thank you!

Speed: All right, so we seem to have clear directives from you. There haven't been any vocalized objections, so I guess what I'd like to ask you, Lyn, is to give us whatever summary remark—actually, what you said to Elliot was pretty clear, but I don't know if you have anything else for us.

LaRouche: Well, simply, we should consider ourselves as in a march, a march for victory, a victory for mankind; a victory for the United States, a victory for the future of mankind in general. And for achieving things as people, which mankind has never successfully done well, so far.

Speed: OK, thank you. I hope we see you next week!

Every Day Counts In Today's Showdown To Save Civilization

That's why you need EIR's **Daily Alert Service**, a strategic overview compiled with the input of Lyndon LaRouche, and delivered to your email 5 days a week.

For example: On Jan. 7, EIR's Daily Alert featured the British hand behind the pattern of global provocations toward war. Of special note is British Intelligence's role in instigating the Saudi Kingdom's attempt to set off a Sunni-Shia war. This religious war has been the intent of British strategy since the Blair-Bush attack on Iraq in 2003.

We also uniquely update you regularly on the progress toward the release of the suppressed 28 pages of the Congressional Inquiry on 9/11, which would expose the Saudi role.

Every edition highlights the reality of the impending financial crash/bail-in policies that would realize the British goal of mass depopulation.

This is intelligence you need to act on, if we are going to survive as a nation and a species. Can you really afford to be without it?

THURSDAY, JANUARY 7, 2016

Volume 2, Number 97

EIR Daily Alert Service

P.O. Box 17390, Washington, DC 20041-0390

- British Crown Pushing War and Genocide in 2016
- Financial Mudslide Goes On; Monetarist Tyranny Gloats over Bail-Ins
- Moody's Downgrades Portugal's Novo Banco
- Puerto Rico's Default: It's Every Vulture for Himself
- Wide Glass-Steagall Debate Set Off Again by Sanders Speech
- MI6 Mouthpiece Evans-Pritchard Touts Persian Gulf Chaos
- North Korea Tests a Miniaturized Hydrogen Bomb
- Uighur Terrorists Found in Indonesia
- Foreign Investors Are Flocking In to China

EDITORIAL

British Crown Pushing War and Genocide in 2016

II. Helga Zepp-LaRouche in Beijing

HELGA ZEPP-LAROUCHE

The New Silk Road Becomes The World Silk Road

Aug. 4—The following speech was delivered by Helga Zepp-LaRouche, founder and chairwoman of the Schiller Institute, on July 29 at the "Think-20" Forum (or T-20 Summit) in Beijing. The Forum was organized by three Chinese think-tanks: the Institute of World Economics and Politics (IWEP) at the Chinese Academy of Social Sciences (CASS), the Shanghai Institutes for International Studies (SIIS), and the Chongyang Institute for Financial Studies at Renmin University of China (RDCY), with the participation of 500 think-tank experts, politicians, and representatives of international organizations from 25 countries, with a view to formulating suggestions to the heads of state and government of the G-20 member countries. Mrs. Zepp-LaRouche spoke on the first panel of the two-day conference dedicated to "Global Governance: System Improving and Capacity Building."

Since the G-20 represents the most powerful combination of industrial and emerging countries on the planet, there is presently no other agency which can address the existential challenges facing civilization and implement solutions to them in time. The populations of most countries have the very real experience of being engulfed in terrifying crises:

• A terrorist threat out of control internationally;

• The migration of millions of people attempting to escape war, hunger and death;

• The resulting refugee crisis that is shaking the foundations of the EU;

• The rise of anti-establishment parties in many countries;

• The Brexit as a warning shot of the potential disintegration of the EU;

• The increasing gap between the wealthy and ever increasing layers of society who are losing their well-earned status as middle class or are living in poverty;

• The experience of the impact of "unorthodox monetary measures" on life savings and expectations for the future;

• The limits of social acceptability of bailout and bail-in measures; and

EIRNS/Stephan Ossenkopp
Helga Zepp-LaRouche delivering her presentation at the T-20 Summit in Beijing, China, July 29, 2016.

• The growing fear that the world has entered a new cold war and a nuclear rearmament spiral—in short, a growing loss of confidence in the establishment of at least the trans-Atlantic sector.

Instead of proposing solutions to these problems, the upcoming G-20 Summit is refusing to acknowledge these crises, in an effort to hide the failures of the dominant policies, in particular since 2008, behind public relations rhetoric, and is failing to take the chance of the upcoming summit to present real solutions to these crises.

As a result, the G-20 Summit will not have effects in the realm of virtual reality, but rather in the realm of history, and in the lives and happiness of billions of real people.

There are immediate solutions at hand, but they require the willingness of leading institutions to revise the axioms of current policies and instead return to policies that have not only proven to be effective in previous times of crisis, but also represent a new paradigm that can lay the basis for the next one hundred years of the human species and beyond.

UNHCR/I. Prickett

Refugees from war and misery in Afghanistan are being deported from an internment camp in Greece in violation of human rights.

To Restore Hope Which Has Been Lost

In order to give hope for a better future for all of mankind, a hope which has been lost in many parts of the world, the G-20 Summit must come forward with a vision that offers a remedy, a pathway to overcome those crises I have mentioned, by establishing a higher level of reason to realize the common aims of humanity.

1. The only "practical" expression of that vision—and that is not a contradiction in terms—is the perspective of the New Silk Road put on the table and implemented for three years now by the Chinese government. As of now, over 70 countries are participating in various aspects of the proposal—such as infrastructure and development projects.

   What China calls "win-win" collaboration in such joint projects is not only the only efficient way to overcome geopolitical confrontation, but is also coherent with the principles of the Peace of Westphalia, according to which any successful order of peace must be based on the "interest of the other."

   Geopolitical confrontation was the root cause of two World Wars in the 20th Century and of the underlying danger of a third, global war today, which, given the existence of thermonuclear weapons, would be a war of annihilation.

   The New Silk Road concept must therefore be extended to all regions of the world as a concrete offer to overcome underdevelopment, as a "World Silk Road."

   If the G-20 member states were to promise to implement such a proposal, with the solemn commitment to overcome hunger and poverty, and provide clean water for everyone within a few years—something which is technologically eminently feasible,— it would cause a revolution of hope and optimism in the world.

2. In order to eliminate both the reasons for mass migration from South-West Asia and Africa, and eliminate the environment for recruitment of terrorists, there must be a comprehensive industrial development perspective, which will rebuild the war-torn regions by means of an integrated plan to develop infrastructure, industry, agriculture, and education, to transform those parts of the world into areas that have increased capacities as a result of a higher productivity of labor power.

   In general, the projects of the World Silk Road

EIRNS/Stephan Ossenkopp

Helga Zepp-LaRouche (third from right) with the other participants in Panel 1 on July 29, the opening day of the T-20 Summit.

must be defined so as to have the optimal impact on the cognitive powers of the populations of the respective countries, in order to facilitate the best possible increase in productivity of the world economy. The focus therefore must not only be on innovation, but on qualitative breakthroughs in the understanding of qualitatively new physical principles of our universe.

Examples of this are crash programs for the development of thermonuclear fusion power, which will provide energy and raw materials security for mankind, as well as the development of new water resources through the peaceful use of nuclear energy for the desalination of large quantities of ocean water, the ionization of moisture in the atmosphere, and other technologically innovative forms.

International cooperation in space research, travel, and colonization defines the pathway for the next necessary breakthroughs in science and technology. It also represents the future-oriented platform for a peace order for the 21st Century. And most importantly, it marks the transformation of the human species toward greater consciousness of its own identity as the only creative species known in the universe so far.

3. An uncontrolled collapse of the financial system of the trans-Atlantic sector would threaten to throw many parts of the world into chaos with unpredictable consequences. The so-called "tool-box" of financial instruments, which was decided upon after the 2008 crises instead of implementing true reforms, has been used up. The consequent "unorthodox monetary instruments," such as quantitative easing, negative interest rates, and helicopter money, have in large part produced the opposite of the intended effect.

The fact that the reintroduction of the FDR Glass-Steagall banking separation law has been adopted in the election platforms of both the Democratic and Republican parties in the United States, and the fact that there is a growing discussion in several European countries about reducing the future risk of the financial system by introducing Glass-Steagall criteria in Europe as well, create a very favorable precondition for agreeing upon a global Glass-Steagall Act at the upcoming G-20 summit.

If the G-20 Summit were to put the World Silk Road on the agenda, the Chinese Dream would become the World Dream.

Zepp-LaRouche Call Resonates at Beijing Think-20 Event

by William Jones

Aug. 5—Speaking on July 29 at the Beijing "Think-20" Summit, where international think-tanks were gathered to elaborate and present proposals for the upcoming G-20 Summit in China September 4-5, Helga Zepp-LaRouche urged that the G-20 must "address the existential challenges facing civilization and implement solutions to them in time." She went on to outline the crises now facing humanity: looming financial collapse, the potential disintegration of the EU, the refugee crisis, and the danger of nuclear war. "The refusal of the upcoming G-20 Summit to acknowledge that situation," Zepp-LaRouche said, "and failure to take the opportunity of the upcoming summit to present real solutions to these crises, will not have effects in the realm of virtual reality, but rather in the realm of real history and in the lives and happiness of real people."

"There are immediate solutions at hand," she said, "but they require the willingness of leading institutions to revise the axioms of current policies and return to policies that have not only proven to be effective in previous situations, but also represent a new paradigm that can lay the basis for the next one hundred years of the human species and beyond."

The two-day Think-20 Summit was sponsored by three of the most prestigious scholarly institutions in China: the Institute of World Economics and Politics under the Chinese Academy of Sciences; the Shanghai Institutes for International Studies; and Renmin University's Chongyang Institute for Financial Studies. Its title was "Building New Global Relationships: New Dynamics, New Vitality, New Prospects," and it included 500 think-tank experts, politicians, and representatives of international organizations from 25 countries.

The Chinese organizers are taking very seriously their responsibility as host of the this year's G-20 summit. The G-20 has effectively become the "steering committee" of the world economy since its establishment after the 1997 financial crisis. China has a program of industrial reconstruction based on the template of its own New Silk Road Initiative; China has therefore placed a focus on the issues of "innova-

EIRNS/Stephan Ossenkopp

Helga Zepp-LaRouche (center) with other participants at the July 29-30, 20016 T-20 Summit.

tion" and "infrastructural investment" at this year's summit.

At the same time, there is a fairly clear understanding on China's part of the serious crisis facing the present world financial system. This was underlined by a number of the Chinese speakers at the opening of the conference. "The world economy is faced with great risks accumulating," said Professor Cai Fang, the vice president of the China Academy of Social Sciences. "We have to be more capable in dealing with volatility. The effect of contagion in the economy has become great," Cai said.

And while the Chinese have underlined the need for a new type of global governance, the G-20 is also composed of countries whose rulers are all too satisfied with the present system of governance. While China and the developing countries would like to see major reforms in the international system, the United States and Europe, the core of the New York-London financial structure, have shown no desire to change the international financial system—or the balance of power supported by that structure.

While the gathering included noted scholars from China, it also attracted activists from various "globalist" organizations internationally, for whom the term "sustainable development" really means "no development." These included graduates of the Club of Rome's zero-growth movements of yesteryear. It also included former government officials and members of international organizations for whom any fundamental change in the present financial order is anathema.

In the few minutes she had for her presentation,

Zepp-LaRouche succeeded in underlining the strategic nature of the Chinese New Silk Road project and the need for both a return to Glass-Steagall bank separation and a crash program for the development of thermonuclear fusion power. The various crises facing humanity today, from the imminent danger of a new financial blowout to the unending flow of war refugees from the Middle East and North Africa into Europe, could only be resolved by concrete action by the G-20 moving in the direction outlined by China, she warned.

Angered by the Truth

The reaction of the other panelists to Zepp-LaRouche's remarks was mixed. Half the panel, in particular the Chinese participants, were very excited that such a perspective was presented by one of the international guests at an otherwise rather tame gathering. A number of panelists, however, were visibly suppressing anger and rage at this disruption of what they hoped would be a carefully "controlled environment," where "sustainability" and "minor system corrections" remained the norm. Yet many from the panel and the audience came up afterward to congratulate and to converse with Mrs. Zepp-LaRouche, who is still known as the "Silk Road Lady" in Chinese circles.

While there was a general consensus at the forum that the present world situation was on the verge of crisis and that the IMF system as it now exists was fundamentally flawed, there were few among the Western participants willing to face the imminent danger of a new financial blowout, or courageous enough to heed the call for a fundamental reform of the world financial system. And while all the Europeans were agitated by the gains being made by the far right parties in many European countries, they failed to see the cause in the absolute failure of the present financial and political structures to meet the needs of their populations.

The Confucian Ideal of Harmony

For most of the foreign delegates it was still "steady as she goes" in the hope that this Titanic of a financial system would ultimately not hit its iceberg. And while the New Silk Road was brought up again and again by the Chinese scholars, most of the panels were characterized by various schemes to provide a "band-aid" for what is fundamentally a failed system.

What is Think-20?

Think-20, also referred to as Think Tank 20, or just T-20 was created in 2011-2012, and is one of seven policy input adjuncts to the G-20; the others are named Business, Civil Society, Youth, Women, Labor, and Innovation. Each G-20 presidency organizes the T-20 function for the year, to provide "the analysis of global think tanks and high-level experts in order to provide analytical depth to ongoing G-20 discussions and produce ideas to help the G-20 on delivering concrete and sustainable policy measures."

Cai Fang (left), vice-president of the Chinese Academy of Social Sciences, in discussion with William Jones, Washington Bureau Chief for the Executive Intelligence Review, *at the T-20 Summit in Beijing, China.*

One of the few exceptions was Vladimir Yakunin, president of the World Public Forum "Dialogue of Civilizations," who complained that there had been no fundamental reform after the 2008 financial blow-out, and that therefore the world was still enveloped in financial turmoil with the danger of a new and greater blow-out ahead of us. He pointed in particular to the lamentable fate of the three million people who are presently starving in Africa.

And then there were those who were totally enraged at the disruption of their illusions by the reality of the crisis. This was dramatically expressed at another panel, where *EIR*'s Bill Jones, part of the three-man Schiller Institute delegation outlining the 40-year battle for a New World Economic Order, also called for the creation of a new financial architecture. When Jones said that "bail-in and bail-out" policies combined with massive austerity would lead to the death of humanity, a member of the German delegation got up and yelled angrily, "We want analysis, not propaganda," and demonstratively stormed out of the session. Jones continued unperturbed, and after the panel many in the audience came up to thank him for his comments.

The Schiller delegation was given major focus by the Chinese media, and gave interviews to China Radio International, CCTV, and the *Hindu Times*, among others. The invitation to the Schiller Institute to attend this event, reflected not only the recognition by the Chinese side of the historical role played by the Institute, and by Helga Zepp-LaRouche personally, in developing the New Silk Road perspective, but also the importance they attributed to the intervention of such an international think-tank as the Schiller Institute into a debate in which most of the international organizations have a diametrically opposed outlook to China's with regard to the direction it intends to give to the G-20 Hangzhou Summit in September. Among the older scholars in the Chinese institutions there is also a broad recognition of Lyndon LaRouche's 40-year battle for the establishment of a new world economic order.

China's perspective was beautifully outlined at the conclusion of the Think-20 Summit by Professor Zhang Yuyan, the Director of the Institute of World Economics and Politics of Chinese Academy of Social Sciences, and the moderator of the two-day event. Professor Zhang referred to the Confucian ideal of harmony as the model for what China wished to achieve coming out of the G-20 summit. While this is a reflection of China's own desire for establishing a "new paradigm" in international relations, the bigwigs of the United States and Europe still wish to cling to the old paradigm of geopolitics, characterized by conflict and war.

And while the themes of "innovation" and "infrastructural investment" have been placed by China at the center of the G-20 Hangzhou Summit, and all the parties are paying lip-service to these themes, the radical environmental and anti-nuclear bias of most of these international organizations, especially those from the United States and Europe, undercuts any possibility of real consensus for wide implementation. The division in the G-20 of developed countries versus developing countries (in which China still includes itself), has yet to be overcome. It is to be hoped that the unfolding financial debacle in Europe and the United States may serve as a catalyst to shake these countries out of their self-induced slumber, and make of the G-20 Hangzhou Summit the type of historical turning point toward a new paradigm in international relations which China hopes to bring about.

The Promise of
A New Financial Architecture

William Jones, Washington Bureau Chief for the Executive Intelligence Review (EIR), *delivered the following remarks at Panel 4 of the Beijing Think-20 (T20) Summit on July 30. Panel 4 was entitled, "South-North Cooperation, South-South Cooperation and Global Economic Governance."*

The creation of the Asian Infrastructure Investment Bank (AIIB) and the BRICS New Development Bank (NDB) represents a watershed moment in the history of the post-war financial system. The final destruction of the Bretton Woods System in 1971, when President Nixon took the dollar off the gold standard, launched the era of the great bubble economy, which at the present moment has created an estimated total debt burden of 2 quadrillion dollars, in a world economy which barely totals 70 trillion dollars per annum, and the world economy is shrinking.

The AIIB and the NDB in combination with the Belt and Road project, now expanded on a broader scale through the BRICS cooperation, has provided a new directionality for the world economy toward the rebuilding and expansion of world infrastructure, which has the potential for lifting the great mass of humanity out of poverty.

While the call for the creation of a new international world order was raised as early as the 1976 UN General Assembly by a number of developing countries, it is only now that we have a clear movement in this direction which is supported by a number of nations representing half of humanity. But none of this can be brought to fruition if the 2 quadrillion dollars of unpayable debt continues to suck dry the trough of existing credit.

And this problem cannot be resolved through any simple "structural reform" or more rigorous tax collection. It will require a fundamental reform of the system, including the elimination of the greater part of outstanding debt which has largely been the result of rampant speculation and even out-and-out thievery.

The only thing that is "too big to fail" is the future of humanity. And if we travel down the same road of "bail-in, bail-out" combined with the drastic austerity measures that we have experienced these last several years, humanity as we know it is seriously at risk.

Bankers must return to financing real production, and speculation should be banned or, at a minimum, the speculators must be forced to swallow their losses. No bail-out for the gambling casino! We must return to bank separation legislation as this was introduced under Franklin Roosevelt with the Glass-Steagall legislation. And we must return to a system of national banking.

The recent creation of the AIIB and the NDB, China's Belt and Road Initiative, and the BRICS collaborative mechanism, are the road to a better future for the countries of the South. But the countries of the North must begin to re-evaluate their own situation. The ongoing collapse of the EU, with or without Brexit, and the devastation of the U.S. economy which has led desperate American voters to seek refuge in the cheap promises of a real estate charlatan, clearly indicate that the London-New York financial system as we have known it, is at an end and no longer corresponds to the needs of the people.

But people tend to stick with what they know rather than venture into what they don't know. In stormy weather, a frightened sailor may cling tightly to the masthead rather than venture into the ocean, even though the ship is sinking, and to continue to cling to it means certain death.

So work must be done to explain the options. But the optimism created by these new institutions and the programs now underway to develop the Belt and Road Initiative, are our best arguments to convince the governments of the world that the Belt and Road has got to be transformed into a World Landbridge, leading to a new phase of economic development in which all nations and all peoples can develop to their full potential.

III. The New Presidency Series

THE NEW PRESIDENCY

A Truly Human Culture: An Expression of the Creative Human Mind

by Kesha Rogers

This is the second in a series of articles being presented by the La-Rouche PAC National Policy Committee, in collaboration with Lyndon LaRouche, as part of his campaign to create a new Presidency over the coming 100 days.

Aug. 8—The New Presidency must be seen as fundamental in the fight to bring about a new paradigm and renaissance for mankind. It must start with the principle of Einstein. It must start with creating a new system that has, in essence, never been thought of before. This new system requires of human society that it foster the creative powers of the human mind. In his article titled, "Society and Personality," Albert Einstein writes, "only the individual can think and thereby create new values for society, nay, even set up new moral standards to which the life of the community conforms. Without creative personalities able to think and judge independently, the upward development of society is as unthinkable as the development of the individual personality without the nourishing soil of the community."[1]

The plasma fusion chamber of the Joint European Torus (JET), a project that collaborates with the International Thermonuclear Experimental Reactor (ITER).

The new paradigm that must be brought about most immediately starts with a return to a concept of real economic value, which rejects the anti-human, anti-science, Malthusian zero growth culture. We must end the culture of degeneracy and economic collapse represented by the murderous drive for war of President Obama, and the continued degeneracy of the dead monetary system. We don't need another stooge for Obama.

---

1. "Society and Personality" is included in *The World As I See It* (1934), the translation of Einstein's *Mein Weltbild*.

We don't need Wall Street clones. The two presidential contenders represent nothing but doom. We must implement Lyndon LaRouche's call for a new conception of progress for mankind, based on the adoption of the four laws he has defined as necessary to save the United States.

Concerning the fourth law, "Adopt a Fusion-Driver 'Crash Program,'" LaRouche writes, "The essential distinction of man from all lower forms of life, hence, in practice, is that it presents the means for the perfection of the specifically affirmative aims and needs of the human individual and social life. This has been an integral part of my campaign to revive the U.S. space program."

"A Fusion economy, is the presently urgent next step, and standard, for man's gains of power within the Solar system, and, later, beyond," LaRouche adds.

The four laws that Mr. LaRouche has laid out represent the pathway out of the escalating global financial crisis and economic breakdown. We must return to the economic outlook underlying the language of the U.S. Constitution, as we find it also in the writings of Alexander Hamilton. And that is the basis for the direction the United States must take now, along with collaboration with leading nations around the world, to reflect once again the outlook of the United States under Presidents John F. Kennedy and Franklin Roosevelt, and as expressed by the founders of the Constitution of the United States—the outlook that inspired nations and peoples around the world. It embodies the idea of economic development and improvement, not just for the progress of one nation, but for all nations.

Crash Fusion Program for a New Paradigm

These Four Laws are critical to understanding the type of economic breakthrough that is necessary to do away with the casino economy, and to bring forth a new paradigm for mankind. These are not just legislative acts to be passed by Congress. We are talking about a transformation in the identity of the human species, whether on or off the planet.

A fusion-driver crash program must be the basis for the space program. The crash fusion program will be the central science-driver program for the efficient develop-

A spacecraft powered by fusion arrives at Mars, as conceived in 2013 by a NASA-funded project of MSNW LLC and the University of Washington. It uses deuterium-tritium fuel in a magneto-inertial fusion system.

ment of the physical economy and the productive and creative potential of mankind throughout the universe.

This central science-driver concept is another key principle of the win-win cooperation of an expanded poly-global world. We are not just talking about development of one planet and collaboration on *this* planet. We are talking about development and collaboration throughout our Solar system. The idea of poly-global development and cooperation was elaborated for the first time—from an earlier seed—by a great German space pioneer, Krafft Ehricke.

The development of space travel and colonization is the expression of a healthy human culture, a culture which rejects the zero-growth form of society that confines humans to one planet, in a state of confined existence, both physically and mentally. The revival of our space program as a national mission, in collaboration with leading nations around the world—most emphatically Russia and China—will prepare a new paradigm for the program of mankind, on and off the planet. It will lay the basis for the development of highly skilled, productive work, which will produce net returns not primarily in monetary and accounting terms, but through an increase in the productive powers of the human mind.

Collaboration among nations, such as we have seen with the space program, paves the way for the new paradigm needed to free mankind from its current state of bestiality. The space program should not be seen as merely a sector of the economy—that one can choose to fund or not. It must be seen as a leading, cutting edge of the future of mankind. Mr. LaRouche's policy for developing a fusion economy includes the space program as a major, essential feature, and conversely, the space program requires fusion power for space colonization and transport. This paradigm starts with the creative potential of the human mind, which is first and foremost the most essential basis for a human economy. We're talking about saving and developing a human economy, not a casino, banking economy.

What we're discussing here is a space era, which has to emerge in the way that Lyndon LaRouche and collaborator German-American space pioneer Krafft Ehricke expressed, over many decades in much of their policies and writings. Mr. LaRouche continues to recognize today, just as Ehricke did prior to his untimely death in 1984, that the space program is an opening to a new Renaissance and to the age of reason.

I think that is where we are today: We must now give birth to an age of reason, to rid ourselves of the prevailing war drive that leads to extinction, to rid ourselves of the policy of bestializing humanity, and to embrace the

true identity of mankind as a truly human species.

Einstein as Exemplar of Our Creative Mind

Ehricke was aware that a fusion science-driver program is necessary for the transformation of the human economy, and that that transformation provides the necessary basis for efficient space travel and colonization. He makes this very clear in his development of a Moon colonization and space travel policy. He writes: "The Universe is run by nuclear energy. Space will be conquered only by manned, nuclear-powered vehicles." For our colony on the Moon, he says, "fusion energy is as indispensable and fundamental as the Sun's energy is for the terrestrial biosphere."

The space program represents the next step in the natural evolution of the human species. Ehricke once said, "You come to understand that Earth and world are no longer synonymous. We no longer live in a closed world of one planet inside a womb of a biosphere. Our world is no more closed than it is flat."

Our world is an open space, he says, and its resources are potentially limitless. It is the human mind that unlocks those unlimited resources.

LaRouche identified the exemplar of that universal quality of the human mind in the personality and genius of Einstein. The creative human mind, fostered by a productive human society, makes the breakthroughs to ensure that we have the resources and the potential for increasing the productive powers of mankind on and off the planet.

Ehricke spoke of the expansion of humankind into space as "world development," as a "positive, peaceful, growth-oriented, macro-sociological project whose goal is to ultimately release humanity from its present parasitic, embryonic bondage in the biospheric womb of one planet. That will demand immense human creativity, courage, and maturity."

The program that LaRouche has laid out is the required measure for lifting mankind into this truly poly-global world. It is the necessary program for defining a new international economic platform that establishes peaceful cooperation among nations—of the type represented by China's development of spacecraft to land on the far side of the Moon. LaRouche's program represents a total shift toward unleashing our unlimited potential for the progress of mankind.

Let's put an end to the ceaseless drive for war that will end in a thermonuclear exchange and the extermination of the human species.

KESHA ROGERS

U.S. Must Lead in Space
In Cooperation with Russia and China

Aug. 5—LaRouche PAC Policy Committee member Kesha Rogers submitted the following op-ed to the Houston Chronicle, *calling on the United States to lead in space exploration. The op-ed is in response to a* Chronicle *editorial that attacks both Hillary Clinton and Donald Trump for not having a vision for space exploration.*

Human space exploration is not merely one program on a buffet table of policies that candidates can pick and choose from. NASA represents the cutting edge of the greatest scientific discoveries. Our space program was based on a policy that sought to improve our knowledge and enable our transformation of our Universe. President John F. Kennedy's mission to land a man on the Moon and return him safely to Earth was more than just an audacious goal; it unleashed technological and scientific breakthroughs that transformed society, utilizing the best talents our nation had to offer.

President Kennedy's vision did not just end with landing a man on the Moon. He called on Congress and the nation to meet national goals including the development of alternate liquid and solid fuel boosters, the Rover nuclear rocket, and space satellites for worldwide communications and many other uses. These goals aimed at unleashing a new era in space exploration, which would increase the creative and productive output of our society, inspire the entire world, and lay the basis for nations to collaborate to achieve the common aims of all mankind.

Keeping these aims in mind, it is not the United States which today is offering the hand of cooperation in the exploration of space, but it is Russia and most importantly China, which has repeatedly offered to collaborate with us on space exploration, including return-

Liu Yang became China's first female astronaut, aboard the Shenzhou-9 space docking mission. Since the June 2012 mission, China has repeatedly offered to collaborate with the United States on space exploration.

ing to the Moon for research and development, and protecting Earth from impacts by asteroids and extreme space weather. China is now taking that mission to the next level, and moving to become the first to land on the far side of the Moon. Here again, space opens the door to peaceful cooperation, even while politicians argue for war, sanctions, and chauvinistic nationalism.

It comes as no surprise that the two Wall Street candidates have no policy with respect to our country's most inspiring legacy of the past 50 years. These candidates have failed to meet the standard set by JFK,— but rather than lower the national debate to their level, we should raise it to his. The responsibility of leadership requires us to go far beyond the immediate crises and challenges of our day, and to look into the future, to imagine what mankind must become, and to take the necessary actions to bring that future into being. This was the leadership that President Kennedy exemplified. That is the leadership we must demand now!

EDITORIAL

Einstein and the New Paradigm

by Benjamin Deniston

Aug. 9—Do you realize the truly historical significance of the present moment? It is beyond what most people have experienced in their lifetimes.

People have to realize, no matter what these fools do—Wall Street, London, Hillary, Obama—their system is going down. They're not going to be able to save it. And the idea of continuing to run their proxy wars and bluffs and intimidation against the emerging, rising system of China and Russia,— that literally means the extinction of mankind.

Look at this moment in historical perspective: For centuries these kinds of things happened—catastrophic and destructive collapses of empires—but the societies re-emerged. Now they're playing the same game, the same old geopolitical imperial game: Who is going to be the dominant force in the world—will London and Wall Street allow their perceived dominance to collapse? Will they try to hold on and attempt to destroy any "threatening" power? What does that mean *today*, at this stage in the development of mankind? *It means annihilation!* We're talking about thermonuclear weapons;

Nagasaki, August 9, 1945, after the dropping of the 21-kiloton plutonium bomb. A Japanese doctor wrote, "It seemed like the end of the world."

we're talking about a level of destruction that has never occurred, something that would wipe out global civilization. It is not inevitable; but it *is* the consequence of the delusion that they can somehow prop up the current system and keep it going.

The *new* paradigm that Lyndon and Helga LaRouche are working to create, centers around the fundamental question: What is the nature of mankind? If you're talking about creating something new—forget trying to fix *this* system—where do you look? You look to science, you look to our understanding about what mankind is. What is mankind's mission? What is mankind's potential? What is mankind's nature as a species?

China's win-win policy is a very strong expression in resonance with that principle. We don't need geopolitics! We don't need this crap any more. There's not a finite supply of wealth on this planet! If you want to act like an imperial fool, of a relic of man that should have been gone centuries ago, that's going to lead to the destruction of mankind in the thermonuclear age. Mankind can continually create orders-of-magnitude leaps in the total wealth available for society, the creation of economic value—but only when we act human. This is what China is doing with its lunar program, going to the back side of the Moon. This is what we could do with the creation of a fusion economy.

People have to put themselves on that level; the present crisis represents the potential for that kind of historic shift. But we need to make that shift, or we're not going to continue to exist. Despite what they teach Americans in so-called education today, there's no steady state in the Universe; there is no principle of equilibrium, only a principle of progress. The Universe is telling mankind, "All right, you've reached this critical point. Are you going to progress and take the next step, or are you going to go the way of the dinosaur, choosing the destiny to which Obama and Hillary are committed?"

No Possible Incremental Rescue

That is the level of qualitative challenge before us, and this perspective is critical to lift people out of the mental gutter created by the media today, the gutter of the elections, the endless propaganda war against Russia and China—it's all insanity. You need an outside—or higher—perspective to grasp the actual historic moment before us. This system is done. This system was done in 2008. This system was known to be doomed when LaRouche presented his Triple Curve in the 1990s. It took a little while to play out, but you didn't think it ended with the 2008 blowout, did you? If you thought the bail-out fixed anything—my God! It's just insanity.

People have got to realize this game is over, and it's up to us to act, in conformity with the reality of this historic moment, and act for the creation of the new orientation.

The needed new paradigm centers around the true nature and destiny of mankind, *which means science.* As Mr. LaRouche has recently emphasized, it means true scientific creativity, of the quality that died with Albert Einstein. Einstein came out of a current of science going back to Cusa and the Renaissance: Cusa's work, then Kepler's, Leibniz's subsequent discoveries, and on through Gauss and Riemann. Einstein came out of this revolutionary Renaissance scientific thinking that was centered on the discovery that the human mind is not just something that objectively figures things out about the Universe: It is the highest expression *of* a creative Universe—it is true *creativity*, nothing less.

That creativity is not deduction; it is not a combination of pre-existing components. It's a human capability for the generation of something fundamentally new which does not derive its existence from lower predicates. That's what the human mind does, that's how the Universe is organized, that's what Einstein understood. He was the last to wage a fight against a fraudulent opposing trend that was taking over science, typified by Bertrand Russell. That insight into what true science is, has been largely lost, except for the activity of Mr. LaRouche and some people he has provoked around these ideas.

True science has to come to the fore again, if we're going to talk about a future for mankind; we uniquely recreate our existence on successively higher levels, something no animal does. But how do we do that? We don't just go find resources. We don't just find things; it's what the human mind does. It's what Einstein did. Einstein shows how mankind completely recreates his existence on higher levels, in more a fundamental resonance with the organization of the Universe. Einstein typifies the true source of human progress.

If we don't consciously have that understanding before us, we are not going to be able to continue this critical process. That is the benchmark for what is needed for society today. In the United States, the relative few of us who are still sane are fighting for the future and collaborating with like-minded elements worldwide.

It is a unifying mission before our entire species right now, to come up to the level of understanding that we are responsible for defending the very existence of humanity, the creative species. It means casting aside the failed leading institutions as a sad relic of history that in the future, we will look back on without regret.